A Big Youth Ministry Topic
in a Single Little Book

THE SKINNY

ON

OUTREACH

Greg Stier

with Theresa Mazza

Group

JESUS-
CENTERED

Guide your entire ministry
toward a passionate
Jesus-centered focus with
this series of innovative
resources. Harness the
power of these dynamic
tools that will help you draw
teenagers and leaders into a
closer orbit around Jesus.

The Skinny on Outreach
© 2015 Greg Stier

group.com
simplyyouthministry.com

Credits
Authors: Greg Stier with Theresa Mazza
Executive Developer: Tim Gilmour
Executive Editor: Rick Lawrence
Chief Creative Officer: Joani Schultz
Editor: Rob Cunningham
Art Director and Cover Art: Veronica Preston
Cover Photography: Rodney Stewart
Production: Joyce Douglas
Project Manager: Stephanie Krajec

Scripture quotations are taken from THE HOLY BIBLE, NEW INTERNATIONAL
VERSION®, NIV® Copyright © 1973, 1978, 1984, 2011 by Biblica, Inc.™ Used by
permission. All rights reserved worldwide.

ISBN 978-1-4707-2088-9
10 9 8 7 6 5 4 3 2 1   21 20 19 18 17 16 15

Printed in the United States of America

ACKNOWLEDGMENTS

A special thanks goes out to Debbie Bresina and Jane Dratz. Both of them have patiently worked through my pile of words to help me formulate something that can truly help youth leaders "gospelize" their teenagers. Their great insights and thought-provoking questions have enabled me to clear the clutter of words to get to the core of what God has called me to write to youth leaders in this little book.

I also want to thank Ralph "Yankee" Arnold, who not only reached my entire family for Christ when I was a kid, but modeled for me what it meant to lead a gospel-advancing ministry. His relentless example of prioritizing evangelism both personally and programmatically catapulted my life toward gospel-advancing youth ministry. Much of the DNA that makes up Dare 2 Share today finds its roots in the youth ministry Yankee led when I was a spastic, twitchy teenager.

Finally, I am deeply grateful to all the Dare 2 Share alumni youth leaders who have tested and implemented the principles in this book in the contexts of their own youth ministries. Their input over the years has been practical. Their stories of life-change have been powerful. Their impact on the next generation has been palpable. I truly thank God to be associated with so many youth leaders who are propelling the message and mission of Jesus in such God-honoring, kingdom-advancing ways. Thanks to all the youth leaders out there grinding it out, trying to reach the next generation.

— **Greg Stier**

THE SKINNY ON

OUTREACH

CONTENTS

THE SKINNY

ON

OUTREACH

BEFORE YOU GET STARTED

The book you're holding might be "skinny," but that's because it's all-muscle. This means that Greg Stier and Theresa Mazza have cut away the fat and focused on the "first things" that make outreach in youth ministry powerful and long-lasting. In our Skinny Books series, we've paired a thought leader (in this case, Greg Stier) with a master practitioner (in this case, Theresa Mazza) as a one-two punch. We want you to be challenged and equipped in both your thinking and your doing.

And, as a bonus, we've added an Introduction written by Dave Rahn that explores outreach through the filter of a Jesus-centered approach to ministry. Jesus-centered is much more than a catchphrase to us—it's a passionate and transformative approach to life and ministry. Dave's Introduction to outreach first appeared in his Group Magazine column, and we couldn't think of a better way to kick off this little book. It's time to get skinny...

—RICK LAWRENCE
Executive Editor of Group Magazine

THE SKINNY ON

OUTREACH

INTRODUCTION

Wouldn't it be great if there were a one-size-fits-all evangelism strategy that unfailingly equipped our students to reach their non-Christian friends for Christ? Well, when students who were unchurched tell us about the chief influences on their decisions to follow Jesus, they're more likely to identify Christian friends than anything else. Knowing this, we often conclude that one of our most effective strategies is to strengthen our students' peer-outreach knowledge and skills.

But what if we concentrated on more than simply training teenagers for evangelism? What if we focused our efforts on immersing them so deeply and thoroughly in the life and worldview of Jesus that every encounter they have with the world is an act of witness?

For 18 years Nancy has opened her home in Indianapolis for a few hours on Sunday nights to seniors during their final high school semester. Her agenda is narrowly focused. She wants to equip graduating seniors with the sort of defensible Jesus-centered worldview that will sustain their faith as they head off to life-challenging experiences at secular universities.

An unexpected result: When students learn to think the way Jesus thinks, it's natural for them to talk with their friends about the relevance of their faith in him. It's hard to curb the conversational enthusiasm of teenagers whose growing love for Jesus is matched by a new ability to see him engaging every aspect of their world. If people perish without a vision, it makes sense that teenagers come alive when their eyes are opened.

Jesus used spittle-laced mud to heal a blind man. What does Nancy do to help her students see with eyes of faith? With the great give-and-take of a Socratic style, she introduces seniors to the idea that worldviews affect how we make sense of everything around us. She uses news headlines, popular music and films and TV shows, and fashion trends to expose students to different worldviews. Teenagers begin to recognize the dichotomy between a Jesus worldview and a conventional worldview. With a new appreciation for what's at stake in the worldview battleground, young people engage in serious discussions invigorated by deep Bible study. They learn what it means that Christ in them is the hope of glory (Colossians 1:27).

The intent of Nancy's ministry is clearly to help Christian students prepare for a future that's right around the corner. It's a deep dive for the treasures of truth that are waiting for them in the person of Jesus. And the unstoppable side effect is that these students learn how to advance their faith with non-Christian friends.

—Dave Rahn
Vice President of Youth For Christ USA

CHAPTER

1

*The
Importance
of
Outreach*

THE SKINNY ON

OUTREACH

"For I am not ashamed of the gospel, because it is the power of God that brings salvation to everyone who believes" (Romans 1:16).

"In the same way, the gospel is bearing fruit and growing throughout the whole world—just as it has been doing among you since the day you heard it and truly understood God's grace" (Colossians 1:6).

Outreach is one of those words that can induce twinges of guilt and waves of excitement, all at the same time. Some youth leaders love it. Others secretly loathe it. Some do it out of a stoic responsibility to the "Great Commission," and some do it out of a genuine excitement about reaching the next generation.

But underneath it all, I am convinced most youth leaders know it's essential that they do it, and they want to be more effective at it.

My prayer is that this "skinny" book will help your youth ministry grow "strong" with teenagers who can experience the love, hope, and forgiveness of Jesus Christ!

WHAT DO I MEAN BY "OUTREACH"?

When I use the word *outreach,* I'm talking specifically about prioritizing evangelism in your youth ministry—making it a priority to share the message of Jesus. While this can range from invitational outreach events to seeing teenagers engage in gospel conversations personally, it's that second category that fuels me most. I believe unleashing your teenagers to reach their peers is the most effective, exciting, and impactful means available for reaching this generation with the gospel!

Is there a time for other kinds of outreach? Yes! Yes! Yes!

We can—and should—provide community outreaches, service projects, and social justice opportunities for our teenagers through our youth ministry efforts. Actually, the more teenagers are involved in community outreach, the more they can reach out with the gospel.

Optimally, the streams of social justice and evangelistic engagement blend together into one mighty river of transformation! I've seen this firsthand in some of the most effective youth ministries across the country. It all works together to transform a community from the inside out—and from the outside in.

With all that said, this book focuses on what it takes to do outreach (in an evangelistic sense) in your youth ministry effectively.

My prayer is that when you finish this book, you'll be able to custom-build your own version of a ministry that prioritizes outreach in a healthy, holistic way into the very DNA of your youth ministry. It was this very kind of "gospelizing"—a term I stole from the famous 19th century preacher Charles Spurgeon—that transformed my life when I was a young man.

The ministry in the suburbs of Denver that so radically changed my life advanced the message of Jesus into other people's lives and into our community with purpose and power. Led by a Southerner who spoke with a drawl but was nicknamed "Yankee," this pastor-meets-youth-pastor-meets-evangelist turned my extended family upside down and inside out with the good news of Jesus.

The gospel literally advanced through my rough-and-tumble urban family like a pro football player through a youth football offensive line. One by one, my tough uncles got tackled and transformed by Jesus.

Yankee explained the message of Jesus to my Uncle Jack, who had done hard time in prison and had a reputation with local thugs and even members of organized crime. When Jack heard this message of grace and was asked if it made sense to him, he yelled, "Hell, yeah!" That was his sinner's prayer!

My Uncle Tommy trusted in Jesus and so did my Uncle Dave. My Uncle Bob went all-in for Jesus after he was arrested and sitting in the back of a squad car. Eventually even my hardened-to-the-gospel Uncle Richard trusted Christ.

But I'll never forget the day that I had one of the ultimate privileges of my life, the honor of leading my mom to Jesus.

I was 15 years old at the time.

Where did I learn to advance the gospel at such a young age? From Yankee and the youth ministry he ran at Colorado Bible Church! From the time I was 11, the church was training, equipping, and unleashing all of us to advance the gospel among our peers.

This is the essence of outreach.

Not to oversimplify, but in the context of youth ministry, outreach is simply reaching out—and equipping our teenagers to do the same—with the hope that only Jesus can offer. This can and should be done both relationally and programmatically.

WHY IS OUTREACH IMPORTANT?

For followers of Jesus, outreach is important for at least three reasons.

Jesus Commands Us to Reach Out

In Matthew 28:18-20, Jesus told his disciples:

> "All authority in heaven and on earth has been given to me. Therefore go and make disciples of all nations, baptizing them in the name of the Father and of the Son and of the Holy Spirit, and teaching them to obey everything I have commanded you. And surely I am with you always, to the very end of the age."

This is the last and lasting mandate of Jesus. In these three verses, Jesus gives us—his followers—our mission, cause, and objective. In the words of Dr. Dann Spader of Sonlife Ministries, the Great Commission from Matthew 28 gives us our mission ("go and make disciples") and the Great Commandment (Matthew 22:36-40) gives us our motive (love God, love others).

Because we love God, we must tell others the good news of his love for them. When we share this love with our lives and our lips—and equip our teenagers to do the same—we are making a difference that starts now and reverberates into eternity. The gospel is that powerful.

Let's say I'm going to the store, and before I head out, I tell my 13-year-old son, Jeremy, to make his bed before I get back. I go to the store and come back about an hour later. Once I'm home I ask him, "Jeremy did you make your bed?" He begins to show me all the other stuff he did. He shows me a picture that he drew. "Nice, Jeremy, but did you make your bed?" Then he shows me an Instagram picture of our wiener dog that he uploaded. "Great, but did you make your bed?" Finally and reluctantly he admits to me that, no, he did not.

In a similar way, Jesus told us that he was going to go away for a little while. And before leaving, he told us to "go and make disciples." When he returns, we can show him all the youth group meetings we pulled off, all the curriculum we taught, and all the camps we attended, but will we be able to tell him confidently that we made disciples?

Compassion Compels Us to Reach Out

In Matthew 9:36, the tax collector turned outreach specialist writes, "When he saw the crowds, he had compassion on them, because they were harassed and helpless, like sheep without a shepherd."

Jesus saw the crowds and his heart was broken. The word *compassion* literally means "to suffer with," in the original Greek. When Jesus gazed at the crowds, his eyes glazed with tears because he could see behind the smiling façades into the broken lives underneath.

In Jesus' culture, if you saw "sheep without a shepherd," you could be sure that sooner or later the sheep would become wolf food. Actually, the image that Jesus paints here is one in which wild animals have encircled the sheep and are plotting their sneak attacks to pluck away one animal at a time.

In the same way Satan, the roaring lion (1 Peter 5:8) and his pride of hungry lionesses (lust of the flesh, lust of the eyes, and the pride of life—1 John 2:16) have encircled our teenagers and are charging them one at a time and dragging them away to destruction. Cutting, partying, depression, addiction, and pornography have turned our teenagers into harassed and helpless lambs, ready for satanic slaughter.

But the gospel is the game changer. It allows teenagers to return to the Shepherd of their souls and live under the gentle guidance and relentless protection that he provides for his lambs. And effective outreach makes the introduction.

True Discipleship Calls Us to Reach Out
Effective discipleship is much more than the successful downloading of truth into the minds of our teenagers.

Your lessons are not flash drives to simply plug into young minds and download content.

Biblical content is meant to be done, not just downloaded. After all, part of Jesus' commission to his followers is "teaching them to obey everything I've commanded you."

Nothing quite does this like outreach. When teenagers engage in relational evangelism, they put into practice almost everything you've taught them in youth group. They pray (because they're probably scared and intimidated). They study God's Word (because they want to know how to answer people's questions). And they worship (because they see the life transformation that takes place when a friend trusts in Jesus).

If you think about it, outreach was the primary discipleship strategy that Jesus practiced with his disciples. He had "meetings" along the way for giving instructions, sharing stories (his parables), and talking with them about their outreach experiences. And within this context, Jesus taught his disciples some powerful theological truths.

In Luke 10, Jesus sent out 72 of his disciples to do outreach, by taking his message to nearby villages and cities. Here's what Luke records upon their return in verses 17-21:

*"The seventy-two returned with joy and said,
'Lord, even the demons submit to us in your
name.' He replied, 'I saw Satan fall like lightning
from heaven. I have given you authority to
trample on snakes and scorpions and to overcome
all the power of the enemy; nothing will harm you.
However, do not rejoice that the spirits submit
to you, but rejoice that your names are written
in heaven.' At that time Jesus, full of joy through
the Holy Spirit, said, 'I praise you, Father, Lord of
heaven and earth, because you have hidden these
things from the wise and learned, and revealed
them to little children. Yes, Father, for this is what
you were pleased to do.' "*

Notice a few things about this passage. First of all, the
disciples were excited. Why? They had just returned
from spreading the message of Jesus! Some people had
mocked and marginalized them, but others responded
to the message. The disciples witnessed firsthand the
power of God, revealed through the life-transforming
message of their Savior and Messiah, Jesus!

In the same way, when our teenagers share the good
news of Jesus, they will be excited and ready to share
stories of what God does. These stories may range from
good to bad to ugly, but all of them will be exciting and
filled with the adrenaline of evangelism!

Also notice in Luke 10 that Jesus calibrated some of the disciples' excitement over the "sizzle" of the physical miracles they witnessed, and pointed them instead to the ultimate miracle of salvation. When our teenagers actively share their faith, they will come back full of questions and ideas. This is an ideal teaching opportunity to take them deeper into God's Word and truth.

I love what Luke records in verse 21: "At that time Jesus, full of joy through the Holy Spirit, said, 'I praise you, Father, Lord of heaven and earth, because you have hidden these things from the wise and learned, and revealed them to little children.' "

It's interesting that the one time we see Jesus described as "full of joy" in the Gospels, it's in the context of his "youth group" being so excited about their outreach experience. In the same way, your heart will be filled with joy as you witness your teenagers, well, witness for Jesus Christ!

And as your teenagers engage their friends with the good news of Jesus, the discipleship process is accelerated in ways you may have never imagined. I can't help but think of Andy McGowan, the youth leader at Immanuel Baptist Church in Kenosha, Wisconsin. When I visited his youth group, I was blown away by my conversations with several teenagers. I met *teenagers* who had been reached by teenagers who had been reached by *other teenagers* in his group.

There was a certain depth and spiritual maturity to the inner core of teenagers I met from his group that night. Connecting with them reinforced the idea that evangelism can drive the discipleship process deeper more quickly. These teenagers were serious about their mission and serious about their service to Christ. And they seemed to be having a blast in the process.

I discovered that it wasn't just Andy. He had passed on this passion for outreach to all of his adult volunteers. Plus, there was an entire network of youth leaders in Kenosha committed to this same gospel-advancing philosophy of youth ministry. The network meetings were steeped in gut-level honesty, passionate intercessory prayer, and powerful brainstorming sessions about how to reach every teen in Kenosha for Jesus.

It seemed like every youth leader in that network innately understood that because their teenagers were on mission with Jesus, they were growing deeply in Jesus.

What is happening in Kenosha, Wisconsin, can happen in your city or town, too. What is happening in Andy's youth group can happen in yours, too—if you're willing to prioritize outreach.

➲ A YOUTH WORKER'S PERSPECTIVE *Theresa Mazza*

For us, outreach isn't just a program piece of our youth ministry; it's an ongoing exchange and discipleship strategy—the kind of relational exchange Jesus had with his closest disciples.

We remind students that advancing the kingdom doesn't mean just leading friends in the sinner's prayer; it means leading their friends beyond a one-time prayer to a life as a disciple. We teach our teenagers to keep the following on their heart and mind as they reach out to their friends:

- *We first decide to follow Jesus by placing our trust and faith in him.*
- *We watch Jesus through Scripture and observe carefully how Jesus lived and loved.*
- *We ask. Teenagers must know that faith begins with questions. God is the answer for every searching heart and soul.*
- *We do. Jesus launched the disciples into action. In the same way, we give students the opportunity to be active disciples, not only learning about God with the knowledge of his love, but also extending his love through service and acts of love and kindness.*

WHAT PEOPLE ARE WE REACHING OUT TO?

Teenagers, of course! Because the vast majority of people who put their faith in Jesus do so by the age of 18, it only makes sense that the church puts the vast majority of its outreach efforts into reaching this crucial and spiritually open demographic.

But it's not only the age demographic that cries out to us; it's also their amazing network of connections. The average teenager has 425 online friends.[1] This means that the potential reach of these teenagers through face-to-face interactions and social media is shockingly large.

Because teenagers can have 100 times more influence on their friends than a stranger does,[2] the best ones to reach teenagers are other teenagers. Imagine the life-transforming impact if you successfully mobilize the teenagers in your youth group to drive gospel conversations in their sphere of influence.

WHEN ARE WE REACHING OUT?

Effective youth leaders are *always* reaching out. They are reaching out in their programs through consistently taking their lessons to the foot of the cross and the empty tomb. They are consistently modeling a lifestyle of relational evangelism. They are consistently inspiring and equipping their teenagers to share the good news of Jesus.

Sadly, many youth leaders view outreach as merely an event or a meeting. These youth leaders encourage their teenagers to invite friends to a monthly (or quarterly, or annual) pizza party, all-nighter, camp, or whatever. Here relationships are built and the message of Jesus is explained.

While these kinds of events are fine and good, they sometimes become a cheap substitute for mobilizing teenagers for relational evangelism. Bottom line: Your teenagers themselves are your biggest and best "outreach event." When youth group participants catch a vision for reaching their friends and begin to see their homeroom class, sports team, and Instagram feed as ongoing opportunities for relational evangelism, they become living, breathing, 24/7 ambassadors for Jesus' message of grace and hope.

WHERE ARE WE REACHING OUT?

Effective outreach happens in the youth room and in the community. It happens at the local school and on the foreign mission field. It happens online and offline. It happens anywhere and everywhere—*if our teenagers are equipped to engage in it.* Their peers who would never set foot in a youth group meeting can hear the gospel from someone they know and trust. Check out the Apostle Paul's perspective on reaching beyond his own direct sphere of influence:

> *"You yourselves are our letter, written on our hearts, known and read by everyone. You show that you are a letter from Christ, the result of our ministry, written not with ink but with the Spirit of the living God, not on tablets of stone but on tablets of human hearts" (2 Corinthians 3:2-3).*

As you help your teenagers become a letter from Christ, "known and read by everybody," you'll be giving them three priceless gifts that will last a lifetime and carry eternal impact...

- Eyes to see the spiritually lost and hurting world around them

- Hearts devoted to following Jesus and sharing his message

- Practical skills for engaging others in spiritual conversations about the gospel of grace

THE SKINNY ON

OUTREACH

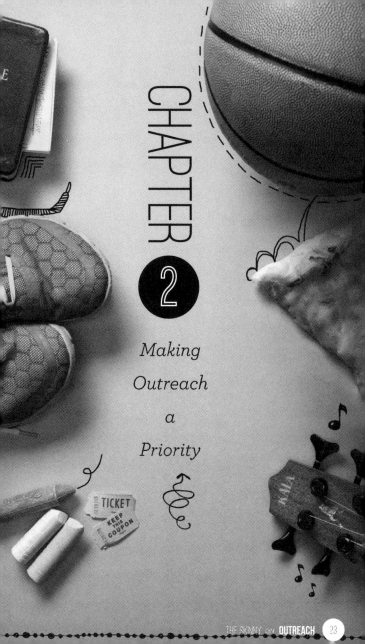

CHAPTER 2

Making Outreach a Priority

THE SKINNY

ON

OUTREACH

Moving your ministry toward a more missional, outreach-focused approach can sometimes feel like you're trying to turn a massive, ocean-going vessel. It doesn't turn on a dime. It takes time. It takes effort. And it takes a powerful engine.

About now, you may be wondering, *how could I ever pull this off?* And I grant you that it can feel like a daunting task—if you think it's all about rolling up your sleeves and making it happen through your own human efforts.

So here's the deal: *You can't do it yourself!* It is the Holy Spirit, the One who dwells inside every follower of Jesus, who will enable you to lead this journey toward outreach-focused youth ministry. He is the powerful engine that must drive any course change.

We can take courage from Jesus: "But you will receive power when the Holy Spirit comes on you; and you will be my witnesses in Jerusalem, and in all Judea and Samaria, and to the ends of the earth" (Acts 1:8).

When the Holy Spirit comes to dwell within us, one of his strong desires is to make us witnesses. And he provides the power for this to happen effectively. Now, don't get me wrong—you are responsible to cast the vision for outreach with your students. You must help them understand what Jesus tells us about sharing the good news and making disciples. And you must train and equip them so that they know the basics of how to conversationally explain the gospel message to others.

But as you cast the vision and challenge teenagers to share their faith, remember that God's Spirit is echoing your challenge from the inside. And even more importantly, he provides the power for them to actually follow through and impact hearts and lives.

So as you set out on this endeavor, ask the Holy Spirit to guide you as you lead your teens into new territory. And rest on Jesus' promise that the Spirit will be involved in the maturation process: "But the Advocate [or "Counselor" or "Helper" in other translations], the Holy Spirit, whom the Father will send in my name, will teach you all things and will remind you of everything I have said to you" (John 14:26).

The Spirit dwells inside every teenager who's a Christ-follower and will be their ultimate teacher. God's Spirit is the engine that drives everything as you set out on this ministry approach full of adventure and kingdom impact.

So with the Holy Spirit as your power source, let's unpack eight practical ideas that will help you prioritize outreach in your youth ministry. These actions will help your students develop a heart for people who are spiritually lost and will equip them with real-world skills to effectively and relationally share the gospel with friends.

Here are some ways our ministry chooses to intentionally partner with the Holy Spirit:

- *There is power in being known. We list all of our students and their parents and divide them among our leadership team. We pray for each individual by name, asking the Holy Spirit for divine revelation and opportunity for partnership, mentorship, and discipleship. As we say people's names, we are partnering with the Holy Spirit in making them known and loved by God, and we begin to connect to them as the Holy Spirit longs to connect with them.*

- *We meet on a regular basis to share insights, praises, and concerns.*

- *We are committed to arriving prepared for each event, program, or Bible study. This gives us extra time to pray and listen instead of running around stressed or handling last-minute prep.*

- *On retreats and trips, we check in with every teenager, especially if they are new or visiting. This gives us a one-on-one opportunity to encourage students and share the gospel. I once did this check-in and found out that a particular teenager had already heard the gospel from a teen in our group and had come to faith in Jesus. I felt a little late and dumb. "Oh Miss Theresa, I asked Jesus into my life a long time ago. Nathan prayed with me."*

#1: PRAY FOR THE SPIRITUALLY LOST

Scripture assures us that something mysterious happens in the spiritual realm when we pray. And while our human reasoning can't entirely grasp how prayer works, Jesus tells us to pray—and to pray specifically for God's kingdom to come. That makes prayer the bedrock foundation for any spiritual endeavor we undertake.

So your first step is to program prayer for spiritually lost people into your personal life, your ministry leadership team, and your youth group meetings.

Start by leading through example. Whether you're opening the youth meeting in prayer, or leading a small group of teenagers, pray for the spiritually lost. Bowed knees for people who don't know Jesus can keep evangelism "top of mind" for teenagers and adult volunteers alike. This doesn't have to take a long time, but this kind of prayer needs to be passionate, powerful, and persistent.

Then, get your teens praying for their spiritually lost friends. A 2010 Barna poll reported that 71 percent of teenagers pray. That seems like a surprisingly high number, doesn't it? It's actually a drop from 81 percent in 1997.[3]

But more importantly, how far do you think your teenagers' prayer scope extends? What kinds of prayers do your young people pray? Are they mostly praying about their own personal stuff? *Help me pass this test. Help me make the team.*

Now don't get me wrong. Jesus taught us to bring our daily concerns to the Father. But he also taught us to do more than that. That's why it's critical that you help your students move beyond their list of personal needs and wants, and guide them toward consistent prayers for God's kingdom to come in the lives of those around them who need Jesus. After all, ultimately, that's what "your kingdom come, your will be done" is about.

Prayer lays the groundwork for getting your teenagers' focus off themselves and onto something and someone bigger: God and his mission to reach people. As your students begin to ask God to bring his rule and reign to their own corner of the world, it will prompt them to think about how they can actively join him in his mission to reach people who are lost and hurting.

But prayer does even more than that! Prayer is so essential and powerful because it connects us to God—his presence, his power, and his wisdom. It opens doors, because it is God who creates opportunities to share the gospel with others.

Scripture tells us that even the great Apostle Paul asked that others be praying alongside him for open doors for Christ's message:

> "Devote yourselves to prayer, being watchful and thankful. And pray for us, too, that God may open a door for our message, so that we may proclaim the mystery of Christ, for which I am in chains" (Colossians 4:2-3).

When I was 15, I heard a quote attributed to Samuel Chadwick, a Methodist pastor in Britain about a century ago, and I've never forgotten it: "Satan laughs at our labor. He mocks all our plans. But he trembles when we pray."

So set aside time in your programming for your teens to pray. Show them how to pray for things of lasting spiritual impact. You may want to even change it up in terms of how you do it each week.

And remember, more is caught than taught. So model how to pray for friends who need Jesus. Let your students know that you are praying for each of them individually, that they would be an effective witness for Jesus in their circles of influence.

➲ A YOUTH WORKER'S PERSPECTIVE *Theresa Mazza*

Teenagers can embrace prayer and experience a deeper connection with God. When this happens, they begin to love their friends and have passion to reach the spiritually lost the way God does. For some students, prayer is a sleepy practice, or they don't understand how to have a conversation with God. Here are some prayer practices we use when we are teaching teenagers to passionately go to God on their friends' behalf:

- **Write letters:** *Verbalizing prayer can be hard. Encourage teenagers to write a letter to Jesus about a specific friend.*

- **Prayer walks:** *Invite students to go on prayer walks with you. Talk to Jesus and to each other as you are moving; this makes prayer active and engaging for teenagers. Soon they will feel ready to go on their own prayer walks and pray for their friends with fervor.*

- **Prayer wall:** *Allow students to write out their prayers. A prayer wall is a good reminder that others are praying for their friends as well.*

- **Standing in:** *Allow teenagers to stand in for someone they are praying for.*

- **Partner up:** *Give students plenty of opportunities to share prayers together.*

#2: INSPIRE YOUR TEENAGERS FOR OUTREACH

As you seek to prioritize outreach in your ministry, it's critical that you help your students see their world with fresh, new eyes.

Most Christian teenagers don't realize that they've been called by Jesus to go on a search-and-rescue mission for people who are spiritually lost. But Jesus' directive to all of his followers is clear: "As the Father has sent me, I am sending you" (John 20:21).

We've already mentioned the most familiar of all outreach passages, the Great Commission in Matthew 28:19-20. I want to encourage you to give your teenagers a fresh way of looking at this grand, sweeping call.

At Dare 2 Share, the ministry I lead, we've found that the phrase "The Great Commission" (first widely used in the 1700s to recruit missionaries to go to far-flung regions of the world), doesn't really resonate with teenagers. When teens hear those words, they think of the 20 percent commission the sales guy just made on their 12-month phone contract. A "commission" is no longer understood to be a resounding call to a grand mission, like it was in the 1700s.

But what does resonate with teenagers these days is the idea of a "cause." Whether it's "Stop Sex Trafficking" or "No More Bullying" or some other worthy social cause, young people are willing to join movements that will make their world a better place.

So I've taken to calling Christ's "cause" of reaching people and making disciples "THE Cause."

One denomination has even nicknamed its outreach campaign #TheHumanRight because "every person has a right to hear the gospel." I love it!

But whether you call it THE Cause, The Human Right, the Great Commission, or something else, in order to effectively mobilize your students for this life-transforming cause, you must help them begin to see their world with Jesus' eyes.

With the help of the Holy Spirit, help them develop a heart for the spiritually lost and for a "lifestyle of evangelism." This is different from "lifestyle evangelism," which is sometimes characterized as simply living a good life, so that eventually people will come up to you and ask you why you're such a good person, allowing you to then step into the opening and share Christ.

In my experience, the "lifestyle evangelism" approach of waiting for people to ask us about Jesus results in a boatload of missed opportunities. I'm convinced, based on my reading of the book of Acts, that this is not what God had in mind.

And it is not how the message of the early church spread like wildfire. Jesus' first followers shared their faith in word AND deed. They simply couldn't keep their mouths shut about Jesus as they lived out their faith on full display via their transformed lives. It takes a both/and approach.

The earliest Christians saw *everyone* around them who didn't know Jesus as hurting and spiritually lost and in desperate need of a Savior. And that's the mindset you need to nurture in your students, so that they start to see themselves as strategically placed by God in a school, neighborhood, sports team, family, and elsewhere, to share the message of Jesus.

Straight from the pages of Scripture, you can cultivate this mindset and unpack a variety of motivations for outreach. These include:

1. **Love for God.** "For Christ's love compels us. ... We are therefore Christ's ambassadors, as though God were making his appeal through

us. We implore you on Christ's behalf: Be reconciled to God" (2 Corinthians 5:14a, 20).

2. **Compassion for the spiritually lost.** "When he [Jesus] saw the crowds, he had compassion on them, because they were harassed and helpless, like sheep without a shepherd" (Matthew 9:36).

3. **Obedience to God.** "For we must all appear before the judgment seat of Christ, so that each of us may receive what is due us for the things done while in the body, whether good or bad. Since, then, we know what it is to fear the Lord, we try to persuade others" (2 Corinthians 5:10-11).

Oh yeah, and hell.

Let's not forget about that. Let's motivate teenagers to rescue their friends from the hell they are headed to and the hell they're going through apart from Jesus Christ.

As you help your teenagers develop a heart for people and a lifestyle of evangelism, they will begin to see sharing their faith as a natural overflow of their relationship with Jesus.

Instead of seeing reaching people with the message of Jesus as an impossible situation, I see it as a series of ongoing opportunities to share the gospel. So how can we inspire teenagers to lead this kind of life?

When I served at Belmont Church in Nashville, we inspired outreach by giving our students a visual. We posted a map of our city and county. We had young people place pins where they lived, and different color pins represented different schools. This way, they could see how many kids from youth group and adults were praying and sharing Christ. This allowed our teenagers to see that they were not in it alone.

We also created a prayer wall. Here students could post prayers for their friends. When a wall is full of prayers, it impresses on teenagers that there is power in prayer, and they are inspired to participate.

#3: TRAIN YOUR TEENAGERS TO PRESENT A CLEAR, COMPELLING GOSPEL MESSAGE

Be honest: How many of your teenagers could clearly explain the good news of Jesus to someone who's never set foot in a church? Even if the opportunity dropped right into their lap, many teenagers have no idea how to explain this message—yet it's the most important message on the planet!

So it's essential that you equip your students with a clear, simple way to share the core essentials of the gospel message.

At Dare 2 Share, we use the GOSPEL acrostic. It goes like this:

G od created us to be with him (Psalm 100:3)

O ur sins separate us from God (Romans 3:23)

S ins cannot be removed by good deeds (Isaiah 64:6)

P aying the price for sin, Jesus died and rose again (Romans 5:8)

E veryone who trusts in him alone has eternal life (John 3:16)

L ife with Jesus starts now and lasts forever (John 10:28)

Keep in mind that the GOSPEL acrostic is not an evangelism script or technique.

It's not a method.

It's a message.

And once your students master it, it enables them to clearly explain the gospel message of grace.

Methods come and go, but the message of Jesus has been with us for 2,000 years. Get teenagers to really master the message first and they can use it with almost any method.

Think of it this way: Learning the six key truths of the GOSPEL is much like putting in the prep work needed to play a guitar. First, you learn the chords. Chords give you the basics, and as you master them, you can be creative and begin to play your own beautiful music.

Similarly, once teenagers learn the "chords" of the GOSPEL acrostic, they can let the Holy Spirit motivate them as they tell people about the gospel in the midst of genuine, relational, give-and-take conversation.

#4: EQUIP YOUR TEENAGERS TO HAVE SPIRITUAL CONVERSATIONS

There's a sense in which a spiritual conversation is like flying on an airplane. Bringing up God is like the takeoff. Talking about Jesus' gospel of grace happens at cruising altitude. Turbulence is when people want to argue or mock you. Landing is wrapping up the conversation and seeing which "landing strip" they will choose.

By coaching your students through this process, you'll help instill the skills and confidence they need to navigate a spiritual conversation from takeoff to touchdown.

So let's start with the takeoff—just bringing it up. Over the years, I've learned that it helps to lead with questions, which is what Jesus himself often did. In Mark 8 alone, Jesus asked 16 questions. Here are just a few:

- "Why does this generation ask for a sign?"

- "Who do people say that I am?"

- "What good is it for someone to gain the whole world, yet forfeit their soul?"

The power of leading with questions is that it unleashes people's natural curiosity and pushes them to think more deeply about what they believe—and why. There's a simple conversational approach that's built on this principle called "Ask, Admire, Admit." Here's how it breaks out:

- **Ask** honest questions. Start with secular stuff, then move to spiritual subjects. Ask questions about what people believe—not to trap them, but to understand them and break down barriers. Asking questions helps you connect and gives you time to pray and ask God for help.

- **Admire** the things you can about what they believe. Focus on areas of commonality, not the areas of difference, so you are building bridges not walls. Even if you can't find anything to admire in their belief system, at least you can admire their honesty in sharing it with you!

- **Admit** your own need for Jesus and explain his message by weaving the GOSPEL acrostic into your conversation. Bring the attitude that you are just "one beggar showing another beggar where to find bread" to this part of your conversation, and share your own faith story.

The process of "Ask, Admire, Admit" gets you from takeoff to cruising altitude, but what about the landing?

It's sometimes the most challenging part of the conversation. So here are two questions that help land the plane:

- **"Does this make sense?"** (If they say "no," explain it again. If they say "yes," ask the next question.)

- **"Is there anything holding you back from trusting in Jesus right now?"** From here the conversation can go one of three ways:

  - *Some people will reject the gospel and mock you.* When this happens, stay calm, speak softly, refuse to argue, and ask questions that make them think.

  - *Some people will be intrigued and want to find out more.* Keep the relationship going, help them find answers to their questions, and keep praying for them.

  - *Some people will be ready to place their trust in Jesus.* Encourage them to receive this free gift right away.

There's a free Dare 2 Share app that has short training videos about navigating these basics, from takeoff to landing. Check it out yourself, and then encourage your teenagers to download it, too.

Simulate conversations about faith and the gospel in a safe environment. Let teenagers think through their response and their approach with you, and with their peers, before they go out and share the gospel. Take them places where these conversations can happen—such as a mall, or skate park. You probably won't choose the public library, but if that's where teens in your area hang out, it might be the best place! In our community of Broomfield, it's Sonic. Recently my friend Jakob took some students to Sonic after youth group, and it was a conversation-rich spot.

When I served at Rocketown in Florida, we invited skaters to come to our student center, but then we realized our skaters had a much better chance at sharing the gospel if we took them to other skate parks. And we were right there with them to encourage them and coach them. So we toured in vans with a bunch of Christ-following skaters and took them to skate parks all over Florida.

We encouraged our teens to always look for opportunities and divine appointments. Where there's a skate park, there are injuries. Our skaters started praying for other teens when they got injured. This often gave them the chance to share the gospel. One student was healed on the spot, and after using some not-so-holy language, he came to skate church where a fellow skater shared the gospel with him.

#5: GIVE YOUR TEENAGERS A FAITH-SHARING STRATEGY

Sometimes it helps to break the faith-sharing process down into more understandable, incremental parts. THE Cause Circle is a simple tool that does just that. The Circle's three basic components—Pray With Passion, Pursue With Love and Persuade With Truth—give students a feel for the steps along the way in this amazing process of introducing others to Jesus.

This tool can make teenagers' interactions more purposeful, because it gets young people thinking about outreach as both a mindset and a process.

So let's unpack each step of THE Cause Circle.

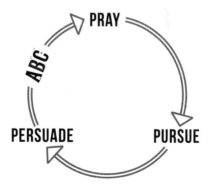

PRAY WITH PASSION

Start by having your teenagers identify a few friends
they want to share the gospel with, and then get them
praying for these friends. As I noted earlier, prayer is the
foundation for everything related to outreach. When you
get your teenagers regularly praying for their friends, all
sorts of good things are set into motion—including the
Holy Spirit's work in hearts and minds!

Plus, when your teens are praying specifically for their
friends, it activates their "faith-sharing radar" to look for
opportunities to bring up Jesus in conversation.

Keep it simple.

Everybody can pray.

No magic formula is needed for praying with passion.
All it takes is a heart for people and an authentic, honest,
open conversation with God, asking him to work in the
lives of our friends. We're called to pray with childlike
faith, which further reflects the pure and simple nature
of this first element of THE Cause Circle.

PURSUE WITH LOVE

You've likely heard the old saying, "I don't care how much you know, until I know how much you care." Wise words for anyone seeking to introduce others to Jesus.

But I have it on even higher authority than this old adage—the Bible tells me so. The familiar passage on love in 1 Corinthians 13 has amazing implications for how we should go about lovingly sharing the gospel. Take your students to this passage using The Message paraphrase. As you read and study it with them, talk about what it looks like to pursue others with love in Jesus' name.

Based on this passage, when our faith-sharing efforts are drenched in *agape* love, they will be determined, selfless, humble, considerate, patient, forgiving, truthful, trusting, positive, all-encompassing, tireless, unswerving, and hope-filled.

Loving acts of kindness and caring are important, but "pursuing someone with love" also includes helping them get to know Jesus and his gospel message. Like 1 Corinthians 13 tells us, love "takes pleasure in the flowering of truth," which opens the way for the next step in the Circle.

➲ A YOUTH WORKER'S PERSPECTIVE *Theresa Mazza*

Fostering a family environment in your youth ministry will train and encourage students to pursue their friends for Christ with love. The family of God looks different from many of our students' families. In this family, we can experience forgiveness, grace, patients, kindness, and unfathomable love. Sadly, I've met a lot of teens who don't go to youth group because they felt judged or unloved. Youth ministry needs to provide the kind of family atmosphere that is like the house where all the kids in the neighborhood go because the fridge is always full and the parents always welcome everyone.

Here are some ways we cultivate a family environment:

- *Leaders are facilitators of conversations and relationships, not adults who always have the answers.*

- *We are bent on inclusion. No one is out of place. We all belong and are worthy. No one is just a friend. Everyone is family.*

- *An atmosphere of trust is built. Teens are not scared away by a sense of judgment but are pulled in by a sense of belonging.*

PERSUADE WITH TRUTH

In our "live-and-let-live" culture, *persuade* is a word that can feel out of synch with embracing diversity and nurturing individuality. But can you think of *anything* in this life (or the next) to which we should more purposefully and relentlessly apply our skills of persuasions than pointing others to Jesus and encouraging them to embrace his gospel message?

The Greek word for *persuade* is used eight different times in the New Testament in direct connection with evangelism. This is not a used car salesman-type pitch, but a sincere yet convincing appeal to a person's heart and mind.

It's the same approach that Paul used when he wrote, "We are therefore Christ's ambassadors, as though God were making his appeal through us. We implore you on Christ's behalf: Be reconciled to God" (2 Corinthians 5:20).

Sure, persuasion can easily become manipulation or coercion if done in the flesh. But when we lay the groundwork of Praying With Passion and Pursuing With Love, then Persuading With Truth can pour forth out of a pure heart that is overflowing with the Spirit of God.

What are we persuading others to embrace? I think of it as the ABCs of disciple-making:

Accept Christ

Belong to a church

Commit to THE Cause of making disciples, too

So help your students learn to Pray, Pursue, Persuade. As you coach them through the three P's, make it clear that seeing the impact in another person's life may take 10 minutes, 10 months, 10 years, or longer.

But with every spiritual interaction, the hope and prayer is that they can gently nudge others toward Jesus.

#6: SHARE STORIES AND SHARE THE GOSPEL

One of the keys to making outreach part of the DNA of your youth group is simply building an ongoing outreach focus into your programming.

Here are three easy programming elements you can build into your weekly youth group meetings.

1. Let Teenagers Tell Stories

Have an open mic for a few minutes each week and invite students to share their stories about living and sharing their faith, regardless of whether their experiences are good, bad, or ugly. Successful or not, the very fact that some of your students are trying to tell people about Jesus can encourage and inspire others to do the same.

Spend time afterward praying for the teens who heard the gospel that week as a result of your students' efforts. Maybe not all of these stories are about sharing faith. Some could be faith-sharing prep stories from teenagers who are at the pray or pursuit stage. They are preparing the way on their knees first.

As someone once said, "We must talk to God about men before we talk to men about God." Other stories may be about how they were mocked for sharing Jesus. But all deserve a hearing, not just the stories of when students radically come to faith in Jesus.

2. Tell Stories

Routinely inspire your teenagers by telling stories of transformed lives as a result of encountering Jesus Christ. Tell stories from the Bible, from church history, and from the teenagers down the street—stories that celebrate Christ in one another.

⊙ A YOUTH WORKER'S PERSPECTIVE *Theresa Mazza*

Give students as many opportunities as possible to share their story and the gospel. In our youth ministry we celebrate God's stories or what we call "God Sightings" almost every time we meet. Sometimes we create our own version of "I Am Second" by filming a student talking about their journey with God and making him first. And we video student interviews in which we ask "What does this faith community mean to you?" and "What was life like before you trusted God?"

We also share testimonies during our worship times together. Often we will connect a student and their testimony to lyrics of a worship song. For instance if we sing "God you're beautiful to me... You can be my King/ Lover of my soul/Cause You mean everything to me," a student might come up afterward and share what it took for them to be able to sing that lyric to God. We choose songs ahead of time and allow students to share how a particular song relates to their faith journey.

We have also made a commitment to create a night that is consistently about sharing story. We choose a student or volunteer to share their story, and then in small groups, the other students are invited to each share their own story.

3. Give the Gospel Weekly

Let the gospel message bleed across everything. Because redemption is the theme of Scripture, *any* lesson can transition into the gospel. Working the gospel into your lesson application each week simply requires a salvation segue or transition statement. Here are a couple of examples of how this works:

- **Self-Image Salvation Segue:** "One of the things that can really help people's self-image is when they find out that someone has sacrificed something for them. I know I definitely feel more valued when I find out someone has done something special for me that cost them a lot. Did you know that the God of the universe made the ultimate sacrifice for you and for me? Here's how it happened..."

- **Anxiety Salvation Segue:** "It's easy to become fearful about the bad things that might happen to us. We could be diagnosed with a deadly disease, injured in a car accident, or killed by a gunman on a shooting rampage. But an amazing thing I've discovered is that while I don't have a lot of control over what happens in this life, I do have a choice in what happens in the afterlife—and so do you. Here's how it works..."

When you give the gospel weekly, both evangelism and discipleship are happening simultaneously! Jesus' message is being shared and you're modeling for your Christ-following students how to take a topic and turn it toward the gospel.

You can also invite and coach individual teens to come up front and deliver the salvation segue and share the GOSPEL acrostic at the end of your meetings. As your teens hear a salvation segue each week, it will help them learn how to think about virtually every conversational topic as an opportunity to point people toward Jesus.

#7: IGNITE YOUR TEENAGERS WITH CATALYTIC EVENTS

Catalytic events can be instrumental in shifting the tone of a group by triggering a spiritual passion in your teenagers—both for God and for their friends who need Jesus. This might be a retreat, an evangelism-focused service project, a mission trip, or a conference.

Here are a few personal stories from students who've had their passion for evangelism kick-started at one of Dare 2 Share's student training conferences.

- "You all changed my life ... I am so sold out to Christ! ... After seeing Jesus save two of my friends this weekend, I can't wait to go and spread the news at my school!!! Thank you so much, Dare 2 Share!!!!!! Praise God and his mighty works!!!!" —Kyle

- "Dare 2 Share not only touched me, but ignited that fire that's in me for God and moved me to start being BOLD and telling people about the gospel with the help of the Holy Spirit!" —Shaunice

- "Thank you guys so much for helping me open my eyes. I believed in God but never really lived my life for him. Now I'm more than willing to help spread the GOSPEL." —Aaron

These stories get me pumped, and they give us a taste of what it looks like when teenagers get motivated and mobilized to take the message of Jesus to their friends and their schools.

When God gets ahold of a teenager's heart, watch out!

Here are some catalytic events I've facilitated that have ignited a passion for outreach in youth ministry...

- **Backyard Campouts:** It doesn't take a big budget to invite teenagers to set up their tents in someone's backyard. Kids invite friends, they end up around the campfire singing all night, and they have the perfect opportunity to build relationships with friends who don't know Jesus.

- **Creative Night/Share Your Gifts Night:** Give teenagers an opportunity to share their gifts from the stage and you'll be amazed how many friends they'll invite. During this event at our church, we always remind kids that God has given each of them incredible gifts and that we are all uniquely made and loved by God.

- **Messy Night:** Ever played Ultimate Octopus? Yes it's just Ultimate Frisbee played with octopus—it's ridiculously messy and it stinks to high heaven, but it's fun (search online for all the details).

- **Christian Concerts:** Maybe this seems old-school, but in my experience music still moves people. You *might be surprised how many regional or local bands want to reach teens with you.*

These events are driven by the mission and objective to let students know they have a Savior. We focus on the objective—to share the gospel—and we consistently give opportunities for invitation. Events are great for attracting students to youth ministry, but a good catalytic event always takes a captive audience and shares the hope of Jesus with them.

#8: MODEL IT

If you're going to be effective in calling your teenagers to take up THE Cause and reach out to people who are spiritually lost, you must be doing it yourself!

As you seek to personally share your faith with others, let your teens in on your efforts by telling them about both the successes and the failures you're experiencing. Use examples from your own life to illustrate and drive home the practical faith-sharing skills discussed in this book.

The thing to remember in this process is that you don't need to be a master evangelist. All you need is to be one step ahead of the teenagers you are leading. Don't present yourself as perfect; your teenagers will appreciate your authenticity and accessibility. As you pray, seek God's wisdom and ask the Lord to live through you. God will help you make an impact.

While you are an especially critical role model, it's also important to get others adults on board. There is nothing like evangelism to rock the proverbial boat. When you start seeing "those kinds of kids" being invited and participating in your youth ministry, the worries and whispers can start. That's why it's vitally important to get key church leaders onboard with this outreach-focused youth ministry approach. Pray that God will grant you favor (and keep praying), and then share your vision for motivating and mobilizing your students for outreach with your church's lead pastor and leaders.

It's also essential that you cast the vision for outreach with your adult sponsors. Again, no worries if they *don't* have the gift of evangelism. Those adults with the gift of evangelism (like me) can sometimes freak teens out. We tell crazy stories of axe-wielding murderers we've led to Christ, and students cheer and clap and then think to themselves, "Are you crazy? I could never do that."

But when a "normal" adult who strives and struggles can model the ongoing process of sharing their faith with their friends, students are filled with courage. They recognize that if those kinds of adults can do it, then maybe they can, too.

The Christ-following parents of students in your youth group also can be tapped to help coach and encourage their teenagers in their outreach efforts. A simple way to do this is to email three or four open-ended questions to parents every week based on your lesson content—questions designed to engage in real conversation, including at least one question that leans toward evangelism. For instance, if a lesson were on sexual purity, questions might include:

- Why does Jesus even care if we're sexually pure?

- Why is it so challenging to stay sexually pure as a teenager in this culture?

- How do you think sexual promiscuity negatively impacts the teenagers at your school who are engaged in it?

- How does choosing to abstain give you an opportunity to share your faith?

When you provide open-ended questions week in and week out, parents become accustomed to talking with their teenagers about sharing their faith.

As you and the other significant Christian adults in their lives model a lifestyle of evangelism, your students will be watching, learning, and developing a heart for the spiritually lost.

Churches want youth pastors who can grow a youth ministry, but churches don't always accept teens in our community who need Jesus and find him through our youth groups. Here are some key things that bring adults onboard with evangelism to teens:

Salvation: *Leaders and adults in the church want to know that kids are being reached for Jesus. I take this as an opportunity to keep them on the hook to reach teenagers with me. Make sure leaders and other adults hear about and see your mission and efforts to introduce students to Jesus. Ask them to join forces with you.*

Safety: *When parents see teenagers that they don't know, they may begin to worry about safety. Parents who are hypersensitive to their kids being around "those kids" may see the adult-to-student ratio as way off—they see lots of "those kids" instead of also seeing a bunch of adults who they know and trust, adults who are investing time and energy in your youth ministry. Invite parents to create a safe youth ministry with you, one that has lots of loving adults around.*

Story: *Share stories with sponsors and church leaders that give them a thirst for reaching teenagers. Josh might look like a kid you don't want your teen around, but if leaders and parents know his background and story, they might see him through a different lens.*

CHAPTER 3

A Few Final "Farming" Reminders

THE SKINNY ON

OUTREACH

Jesus ministered in an agrarian culture, so he often used farming as an example of the evangelistic process. His disciples understood the analogy, because it was an essential part of their culture. So here are a few farming analogies that may help you as you seek to reap a spiritual harvest among your teenagers.

DON'T GIVE UP DURING PLANTING SEASON

"Let us not become weary in doing good, for at the proper time we will reap a harvest if we do not give up" (Galatians 6:9).

First comes the cultivating of the land, then comes the planting of the seed, and finally comes the reaping of the harvest. Sonlife, a disciple-multiplying ministry, refers to this process as "spiritual CPR" (Cultivate, Plant, Reap), because what's true of planting wheat or corn is also true of planting gospel seeds.

Look at getting evangelism into the DNA of your youth ministry more like long-haul farming, instead of a quick fix series of one-time events. Events are *part* of the process, but events cannot *replace* the process.

So start cultivating the ground through prayer, spreading the seeds through evangelism, and waiting on the Lord. Ask God to move in the hearts of your teenagers to join you because of the immensity of the task. As Jesus said in Matthew 9:37-38, "The harvest is plentiful but the workers are few. Ask the Lord of the harvest, therefore, to send out workers into his harvest field."

And don't give up. Keep striving in the power of the Holy Spirit until the crop comes in!

PLANT WITH PURE SEED

To continue the farming analogy further, remember that the purer the seed, the better the results. It's a basic law of farming: Pure Seed = Strong Harvest.

According to the Food and Agriculture Organization of the United Nations:

> "The use of good quality seed is a prerequisite for the satisfactory production of a good quality crop and is essential for export markets. The following points should be taken into account when considering seed quality:
>
> - Trueness to type (often referred to as variety purity).
>
> - Satisfactory germination and vigor.
>
> - Freedom from other materials, including plant debris, dead or broken seeds, seeds of other

crops, weed seeds, noxious and parasitic weed seeds...

- Freedom from seed-borne pests and diseases."[4]

Too many times, too many gospel presentations contain debris, weeds, and pesticides. They have subtle strands of salvation by works protruding from them, which a spiritually lost person can hold on to for self-salvation. This "grace+works" hybrid is confusing at best, and damning at worst. Paul was so against sowing this brand of seed that in Galatians 1:8 he wrote these words to his fellow spiritual farmers: "But even if we or an angel from heaven should preach a gospel other than the one we preached to you, let them be under God's curse!"

He is basically saying (my paraphrase), "I don't care if Michael the Archangel himself starts sowing gospel seeds that are not up to par, or even me or Luke or Timothy—reject those bad seeds!"

If we keep our message pure by focusing on what Jesus has done for us and not what we think we must do for him, then we will have a bigger and better harvest. Salvation is a free gift made possible by God's grace when we simply trust in Jesus, based on his death in our place, for our sins. This reality is what makes a seed good, pure, and productive.

Remember...Pure Seed = Strong Harvest.

So how pure are the gospel seeds you are planting among your teenagers? Does your gospel presentation focus on our efforts (turn, try, cry), or what Jesus has done?

I strongly encourage you to evaluate the message you are sharing with your teenagers, to make sure it focuses fully on faith alone, in Christ alone. As Ephesians 2:8-9 reminds us, "For it is by grace you have been saved, through faith—and this is not from yourselves, it is the gift of God—not by works, so that no one can boast."

GET READY FOR TROUBLE

Jesus cautioned his followers to expect that neither sowing nor reaping would necessarily be easy. A parable from Jesus in Matthew 13:24-29 provides us with valuable insights we would be wise to keep in mind:

> *"The kingdom of heaven is like a man who sowed good seed in his field. But while everyone was sleeping, his enemy came and sowed weeds among the wheat, and went away. When the wheat sprouted and formed heads, then the weeds also appeared.*

> *"The owner's servants came to him and said, 'Sir, didn't you sow good seed in your field? Where then did the weeds come from?'*

" 'An enemy did this,' he replied.

*"The servants asked him, 'Do you want us to go
and pull them up?'*

*" 'No,' he answered, 'because while you are pulling
the weeds, you may uproot the wheat with them.' "*

Satan has a farming plan, too. He wants to wreck yours.
He is busy sowing seeds of doubt and seeds of discord,
hoping for a harvest of destruction and disillusionment
in your life and in your youth group.

I'll never forget working for a long time in a youth group
as a youth leader, with little to show for my efforts.
Satan was sowing seeds of discord in our church and
discouragement in my soul. But I found my strength in
God, and continued to sow seeds.

Slowly and surely, the harvest began to appear. It was
messy. It was amazing.

In the first chapter of the second letter that he wrote
to Timothy, Paul challenged his younger protégé to get
ready for trouble:

> *"For this reason I remind you to fan into flame the gift of God, which is in you through the laying on of my hands. For the Spirit God gave us does not make us timid, but gives us power, love and self-discipline. So do not be ashamed of the testimony about our Lord or of me his prisoner. Rather, join with me in suffering for the gospel, by the power of God"* (2 Timothy 1:6-8).

To join Jesus in the quest to reach a spiritually lost generation is to join with him "in suffering for the gospel," and we can be victorious if we keep moving forward in "the power of God."

If you're a youth leader who has not made evangelism a priority in your youth group, will you join Jesus in the quest for the unreached teenagers in your community? Will you show your teenagers how, by modeling a lifestyle of evangelism and by training them to share the good news of Jesus with both their lives and their lips?

If you're a youth leader who has made evangelism a priority, will you keep pressing on, chucking seeds, and raising up an army of "seed chuckers," until every last teenager in your community has had an opportunity to be transformed by Jesus?

I can't help but think of John. I met him while on a family vacation to Florida. He was discouraged and disillusioned by youth ministry. He admitted to me that he had no idea why God called him from Chicago to this very small, very old, and very self-focused church in this small beach town on the east coast of Florida.

My advice was nothing new or flashy. I didn't tell him to get a new youth room and have some big event. Instead, I challenged him to pray for his teenagers. He told me he had only five of them, and they all were spiritually lost.

I challenged him to pray for them, and share the good news of Jesus with them until they believed. And once they believed, then his challenge was to help them grow in Christ, and go out and reach their friends for Christ!

John took my advice seriously. Every Thursday, for two hours, John prayed for those five teenagers. One by one, they came to Jesus. They began to grow in Christ. They began to go for Christ. They went to their friends with their newfound message of hope in Jesus, and shared the good news with them. John coached them every step of the way.

As the youth group grew larger, and he got busier, he realized that two hours of prayer weekly was not enough.

He began to go on prayer walks every day for an hour a pop. He prayed and walked, and prayed and walked. He walked so much that he lost 25 pounds. He prayed so much that he gained 50 teenagers.

That's right: 50 teenagers who ALL came to Jesus as a result of John reaching teenagers, and then equipping these teenagers to reach others.

Did it all end happily? Sadly, no. John eventually got fired for making outreach a priority in a church that was against it.

But since then, John has become a church planter. Some of the teenagers in his old youth group (who have since graduated) are helping him plant a church in Orlando. From the ashes of a youth ministry firing, a gospel-advancing, discipling, multiplying church is rising!

If John can do it, then you can do it through the power of Christ.

Maybe it's time for a prayer walk. What do you say?

ENDNOTES

[1] Shawn Knight, "Survey: The average teenager has more than 425 Facebook friends," Techspot.com, techspot.com/news/52665-survey-the-average-teenager-has-more-than-425-facebook-friends.html; posted May 22, 2013, and accessed February 24, 2015.

[2] Pan Hui and Sonja Buchegger, "Groupthink and Peer Pressure: Social Influence in Online Social Network Groups," 2012 IEEE/ACM International Conference on Advances in Social Networks Analysis and Mining, 53-59; 2009 International Conference on Advances in Social Network Analysis and Mining, 2009.

[3] Barna Group, "The Spiritual Activities of American Teenagers," barna.org/teens-next-gen-articles/403-how-teenagers-faith-practices-are-changing; posted July 12, 2010, and accessed February 24, 2015.

[4] Food and Agricultural Organization of the United Nations, "The Importance of Good Quality Seed," fao.org/docrep/007/y5259e/y5259e03.htm; accessed February 24, 2015.